WHO SAYS YOUR FUTURE DICTATES ON YOUR PAST?

Each Step Will Bring You Closer to Your Destiny

Apostle Jean S. Dieudonne

Scripture taken from the HOLY BIBLE, NEW INTERNATIONAL VERSION®. Copyright © 1973, 1978, 1984 Biblica.
The "NIV" and "New International Version"

ISBN # 9780615643250

Apostle Jean S. Dieudonne
www.demonstrationministry.org
P.o. Box 384 Boynton Beach, Fl 33425

DEDICATION

Words cannot express the joy I have in my heart at this moment, with one more reason for me to thank and praise God for His mercy and grace toward me. I praise God the Father, the Son, and the Holy Spirit for using me to share God's heart through this book.

I don't know how to thank my precious wife for believing and supporting me in every step of the writing process. I'm very blessed and thankful for her support of my ministry and all God has planned for the future. It's only by God's grace that I found such a fine life partner.

I also thank Him for my older sister who supported me during the writing process; she was there to push me when I wanted to quit. I also want to thank my mom, my little sister, and my brother as well, for always being there for me.

I dedicate this book to those of you who want to understand God in another, far deeper dimension. I believe you will be blessed by the revelations God has given me to share. May God bless you as you seek Him.

ACKNOWLEDGMENTS

I thank God for my dear Brother Prophet Kervin Dieudonne who has always been there for me, along this journey

I thank God for placing on my path, Deliverance Ministries' overseer Apostle Gene Moody for my Pastoral and Apostolic ordination

I thank God for Prophet Sylverster Ofori for always being there for my family and I spiritually

I thank God for Evangelist Germain Robenson for supporting my ministry.

I praise God for my Dear Friend and Pastor, Roland Oriental, who has been a constant blessing in my life and in my ministry

I thank God for the Baczewski family, who have supported my family and me for quite some time. Words cannot express my gratitude for this family.

Lastly, I thank God for every member of Demonstration Ministry for standing by me, to support me in building the Kingdom of God.

.

CONTENTS

INTRODUCTION

I've written about my personal life in order to encourage others to look at life from a completely new perspective. Perhaps you feel as if you've made too many mistakes and will never overcome them. Or perhaps you've always felt like a victim. Well, I want you to know that the past doesn't have to dictate your future. The person you see when you look in the mirror can go either way. You were actually created to follow the will of God, but you have a choice, and can either follow the lead of the Holy Spirit, or be led by evil spirits. And while that may sound strange, the truth is that though we think we are in charge and dictating our own path, if we aren't following God, we are following the devil by default.

The Bible says that God works everything for the good of those who love Him. Although things may seem tough, if we can only look at circumstances through God's eyes, we will become wiser, stronger, and better able to handle whatever life throws at us. I pray that these revelations will open the eyes of your understanding and help you to visualize things from God's perspective.

There is something I want to ask of my readers. I want each one of you to open your heart, to determine whether or not you are truly a child of God, because that is absolutely the most important decision you'll ever make. The answer to that question will determine where you spend eternity. I, myself have been in church all my life and thought I was a Christian, but the truth is that I didn't know God. Oh, I knew that Jesus died for me and had acquired a great deal of information about God, Jesus, and the Holy Spirit, but I had no personal revelation. I didn't know that I had to make Jesus my Savior and my Lord.

For a good part of my life I looked at everything through the lens of religion (more like a story than actual fact) without realizing that salvation required relationship. Church was merely a habit, much like any other cultural event. I went to church thinking I was a worshipper, but my worship was worthless to God at the time, because I only knew facts *about* Him. Matthew 15: 9 tells us: "Their worship of me is worthless. The things they teach are only human rules.") I understood the natural part (human rules) pretty well, but God is spirit and I had no idea how to know how to be connected to Him in the spirit.

I hope you will keep an open mind, and be willing to learn something good because nothing can get through to you unless you're open to it. If your mind struggles to accept some of these scriptural truths, pray and ask the Holy Spirit to help and clarify. I will back up the tough statements with scriptural documentation. Remember God has no limits; the fact that we have never known or experienced something doesn't mean it isn't so.

Remember, do not rely on what you've heard others say about God or Jesus, but look at their lifestyle and their experiences to discern the truth. Scripture says we will know a tree by its fruits. Jesus never ordered anyone around. He only told them to follow Him, and to do what He did. God is real, so you can ask Him to reveal Himself to you to confirm to your heart that He is alive and well on Planet Earth, and that He loves you. That He is who He says He is, and does what He says He does.

WHY CAN'T WE UNDERSTAND GOD?

The problem is that we, who are mere finite human beings, try to define an infinite, unexplainable God despite of our limited intelligence and vocabulary. Most of the time, we say we have faith in God, but that faith is limited because we are limited by our human experiences and expectations, and we don't know God as God. Our imagination restricts our understanding so that we tend to see God as a superhero, or a powerful being. According to the spiritual laws, God cannot and will not move in a level higher than our limitations, imaginations, or our faith allow Him to go. Limitation is what stops us from seeing God in His entirety. They only allow us to compare God to a limited source.

Scientists try to define the earth; they do all kind of studies in order to understand the earth, but none of them is ever able to fully describe God's marvelous creation. I have never seen anyone clearly describe heaven, or even talk about its length or height. The reason why is because we have limited understanding. If it is impossible to define God's earth, how can one define God Himself? The sad truth is that we *confine* God every time we try to define Him with our limited human minds.

In order to define someone or something, one must start from a starting point of what we know in order to expand our definition. So where on earth do we start to define, describe, identify, and characterize the Lord God Almighty when we have nothing with which to compare Him? The truth is that God can only be revealed to us by His Spirit, and only to those He wants to know Him.

There is a saying in America: "If it isn't broken, don't fix it." Why then would God send Jesus to earth to die if things were so great between humanity and God?

Jesus came to show us the way to the Father (See John 14:8&11). Before His arrival the system wasn't working well because we couldn't understand or relate to a holy God. Even the greatest prophets who ever lived struggled to understand the ways of God. Jesus made a statement that confirms this in Matt. 11:11-12. He said, "I tell you the truth: among those born of women there has not risen anyone greater than John the Baptist. Yet he who is least in the kingdom of heaven is greater than he. From the days of John the Baptist until now the kingdom of heaven has been forcefully advancing, and forceful men lay hold of it."

If John was greater than all the great prophets who spoke in the Old Testament, something had to be wrong with the system. And although John was greater, he was less than the least of us because we have the new agreement (also called the New Covenant) that can help us to understand our God better. Now that we have the Holy Spirit and the New Covenant, we have a clear path to follow. In fact, by revelation we can now know the truth, and experience the life which is Jesus Christ. (See John 14:6.)

Once we grasp the truth that we are limited in our understanding of the things of God, we realize we need Him to reveal the infinite knowledge that only comes by the power of the Holy Spirit. His knowledge is so immense and so far above us that apart from Him none of the things of God will ever make sense, and yet, with His revelation, it will all make perfect sense.

1 Corinthians 1:25 explains it this way: "Even the foolishness of God is wiser than human wisdom."

What does that mean? In order for us to understand the limitlessness of God, He uses foolishness and still gets better results that human wisdom could never attain.

Jesus asked a cripple to get up and walk. It may sound foolish, but it got results. Human wisdom wouldn't know what to say to make a cripple walk. Clearly, human beings are incredibly handicapped by limitations.

Not long ago, the Lord showed me a vision that clarified the issue of human limitations. In the vision I saw boxes inside of boxes ranging from quite small to very large. The boxes represent our limitations; some of us have tiny boxes which can only hold a small amount, while others of us are more open with bigger boxes that are able to receive more truth. And yet outside of our boxes are the infinite wisdom and knowledge that belong to God.

Often we fill our boxes with turmoil and worry, upset by so many things that there is no space left for God's grace to enter or for Him to move.

God is almighty, and nothing is impossible with God, but He is a gentleman, who will never go where He is not invited. That means He cannot and will not wade through the many things in our boxes to help us without permission. And though He's more than ready and willing to come to our aid, it's up to us to ask for His help.

I
MY CALLING

At the age of fifteen I was lying on my twin bed when I heard a voice that sounded just like my father's. So, I got up and went to my father's room, and said, "Yes, Daddy?" He replied, "I didn't call you." I knew I wasn't mistaken because I knew what I'd heard, but because I had no other explanation I let it go and went back to bed.

Two minutes later, I heard the same voice repeat my name: "Jean, Jean." ...Once again it sounded like my father's voice was coming from his bedroom. So, I got up again and went to him. I said, "Yes, Daddy? I heard you call me again." He said, "I didn't call you. It's late so just go back to bed." I went to bed again thinking it was odd. The same thing happened a third time and I could only wonder what kind of game my father was playing, because the third time he called so loud that he could've awakened the whole house. At least that's the way it seemed to me, though at the time it didn't occur to me that my brother, who was also in the room, hadn't heard a thing. Once again I went to my father, who said he hadn't called me. He also asked why I kept coming back.

As I was turning to go back to bed he said, "Wait, Jean. If you hear the voice again, say: 'Speak, Lord, for your servant is listening.'" I returned to bed, feeling anxious, because the familiar story of Samuel suddenly ran through my head. It's not like I hadn't known it before, but I hadn't thought of it when I heard the voice calling my name. A terrifying thought did occur to me at that instant--perhaps my parents were giving me away to someone to serve the Lord, just as Samuel's mother had. As I lay on my bed I crossed my fingers and repeated the phrase, "Please don't talk to me. Please don't talk to me." I only said that because I was so frightened and didn't know what to expect.

That night really got me thinking about my future. I knew for sure that God really wanted to use me. The voice I heard completely captured my focus. It felt like someone was following my every move. I would know certain things on my own, thinking it was normal with no idea that God was working through me and wanted to use me for His kingdom. At that point I wanted nothing to do with church and had no intention of responding to God's call. In fact, because I didn't accept that call, many things started to turn upside down for me and around me.

I was almost sixteen when the devil came to me one afternoon, and I thought he was going to kill me. I saw a big head without a body. I wasn't frightened because I believed that God was protecting me. He said: "I will eat you." It seemed like I must be hallucinating, but I absolutely know what I saw and heard. The bodiless spirit suddenly grew bigger. At that time, I didn't think about it, but it was definitely a real, 3D image. Every time it opened its mouth to speak, it grew larger and then reverted back to its original size. It repeated this process over and over again. I thought, *If that demon could hurt me, he would have done it already.* It was clear to me that though he couldn't hurt me this demon was unhappy with me. Well, I finally became annoyed; enough was enough. I said, "You need to go in Jesus name," but nothing happened.

Then I said, "I'm going to sit down in this bed, and you'd better be gone right this minute." All of the sudden, I felt peace, and it was gone. But that was only the beginning of my troubles. Every time something happened I called on God and He saved me, and yet it never occurred to me to pray and thank Him.

In the same season (meaning the time of persecutions) my dad decided to go to one of the major voodoo places in Haiti to challenge the local voodoo priest. Every year they hold a hugs festival, and people show up from everywhere in Haiti and some other countries as well to celebrate and to renew their contracts. During that period of time, that little town is under the tremendous spirit domination, and I mean literally. As tourists go around town, a spirit may claim anyone and make him do whatever it desires. In fact, as odd as it sounds, he calls that person his horse. We all know that people ride horses, but in this case the demons rode the people. Sometimes, a demon would make a person climb a thorn tree, and when that person got to the very top it would abandon him. Many evil things were happening in that town.

Some people were telling my father not to go, but he said he had to go as a servant of the great Jehovah, because the town had to be set free from those spirits. Word got out to the voodoo priests who were waiting for him that day. I remember we were in constant prayer, and the attacks were coming back to back. It became so hard that my parents had to get the church's prayer warriors to cover them in prayer twenty-four hours a day.

When the day came, we walked to that town because that's how the spirits there would pick a "horse." In that atmosphere it felt strange walking around telling the people about Jesus, until we met with a young guy named Antoine, who was the son of the main voodoo leader. As we were talking to him, the Holy Spirit touched him, and he accepted Jesus right then and there. My dad decided to take him back with us, worried about what would become of him if we left him behind.

When we got back, my dad questioned him, and he told us why he had decided to follow Jesus. He said that, for the first time ever, the spirits had not shown up that day, and in fact, nothing had happened the way it usually did. He was a witness that everything was really different. His father had even called up the spirits and they told him that they couldn't show up because they were ordered not to. The young man said he grew up in that place, and he never saw anyone mess around with those spirits, including his own father. If anyone did something against the spirits, they would severely punish that person. Sometimes, the guilty one's whole family paid the price through death. If it was a minor infraction such as going to church or reading a Bible, they would punish the culprit by asking him to bring 101 different kinds of drinks (not including water), which was nearly impossible to find in such a small, poor country. If the person didn't meet the deadline, the punishment became even more severe.

Many people really wanted to leave that place, but the spirits warned them of what would happen if they ever did. He mentioned that if we usually prayed for one hour, to please pray for two hours, and he asked us to teach him how to pray, too.

It was a month later when I realized how serious the situation really was. At that point I had two things to worry about-- the demon face that I didn't want to see again and what the man said about them attacking us back.

After our grand victory, we thanked God, and after a little while we really had no desire to pray the way we had previously. We were happy, celebrating like it was all over, and everything seemed to be peaceful, before the enemy began to attack in very strange ways.

There was one thing that was very strange, and many others witnessed it, too. For no apparent reason roaches will fill my bedroom every Thursday. I used to sleep in the same room as my older brother, and we would find roaches everywhere. In fact, there were so many roaches that we couldn't sleep at all, and the strangest thing was that, when we tried to kill them, they would simply disappear. My mom and other people would come to help, and every time we stepped on one, it was as if we stepped on nothing. Basically, we had a room full of roaches that we couldn't kill, but only on Thursdays.

But that was only the beginning. As strange as it sounds, I wasn't at all frightened, because I knew from the experience that I had with the demon face that he had no real power over me.

The enemy never attacks when we are strong or when we are spiritually focused. He will use someone or something to distract us in order to pull us out of God's presence. What does it mean to be spiritually strong? In this case, the term "strong" describes someone who is on the same side as God. (See Romans 8:28-31, Psalm 27:1.) Someone who is following the footsteps of Jesus or in the Word of God will always be strong enough to reject demonic attacks. The enemy works in very tricky ways, always attacking when we least expect it. Every time we allow the enemy to draw us away from God's presence he strikes because we are weak when we stray from the Secret

Place. And though Satan is always working against us our victory is guaranteed as long as we dwell in God's presence.

After a while I thought everything calmed down, so I got back to my regular life doing what I used to do. It seemed as if the trials were over. One thing I didn't realize--during my trials, I had no friends. Those I had considered as friend were not there when things were crazy. I didn't have anyone to rely on in those moments until things returned to normal.

One day I went to school, and that day was only a half day because exam time was quickly approaching. That day we only went to the school to get our exam schedule, (in Haiti school is all about memorization), so they let us go early that day and gave us a few days before the exam because we had many chapters to memorize.

My friends and I took the opportunity of the time off to go and play basketball. We knew that as soon as we got home our parents who already knew the drill would make sure that we studied. And some parents were so strict that they would make sure their children knew every chapter line-by- line before they even let them eat.

So, right after school, five of us headed to a nearby basket-ball court, to have fun. We chose sides to play, but since there were five of us, and we were going to play two against two, while the fifth man would have to sit out and sub for anyone who got tired. Once we arrived we saw one of our friends lying in the middle of the court, so we politely asked him to leave the court so we could play, but he didn't respond or move at all. We thought he must've wanted to play awfully bad to do that.

We decided to move the game to the other side of the court. As we were walking we saw water on the court, and we knew it wasn't raining, and we hadn't brought any water. As we looked back the water was filling the area underneath our friend who was lying on the court.

That's when we ran back to him and started to shake him, but he didn't respond at all. My friends were so terrified that they ran away and left me alone with him. I was screaming at them to please come and help me, but they were too frightened to help.

So, I carried him myself, about 800 to 1000 feet back to my house, too far from other homes where I might have gotten help along the way. I had to cross a soccer field carrying someone that was I later learned was dead, but seemed alive to me. At that time, I understood little about unnatural death.

When I got home with him, they called medics to come and check him out, and they said he must have been dead for a while because he had already turned blue. When I heard that I went to look at him, and he appeared alive, as if he was trying to say something, but I didn't know how to explain that I knew he was alive because I had seen him move. I knew that no one would believe me, because they were all so fearful.

The point is that these things troubled me tremendously because I couldn't understand why no one else saw what I saw. I knew I had often heard God speak to me. How did others deal with such things? I had questions about many things, but I wasn't getting much in the way of answers. Remember that I was called by God at age fifteen, but chose to run my own life. So, basically as I was playing around, God allowed such things to happen around me and even allowed my close friend to die in order to show me my destiny. There I was anointed of God and yet unable to help him. This thing troubled my conscience for many years. I learned a valuable lesson that day.

To be perfectly honest I didn't really understand that lesson until the age of twenty-five--the age I finally answered God's call. At that point God took me back through my past and started showing me things that happened starting the day I had refused His call. I saw many things that had happened to me and other people that I could have prevented if I had said yes to Him that day. My friend's death was a good example, but it certainly wasn't the only one. If I had only chosen to follow God that day, I strongly believe things would have been different for my friend.

I want to share something I learned from that experience. There is a way out of every challenge or situation we face in our lives. The things that God asks us to do on a daily basis are usually meant to protect us from falling into traps of one kind or another. For example: Say I feel that I must pray or go to church, but for some reason I choose not to obey. If I fail to realize that the time was to prepare me and protect me during an upcoming moment of hardship I end up suffering from a lack of preparation.

The Lord took me to the Bible, and I was reading how hard it was for Moses, but he left everything behind to answer God's call. If he had rejected it the way I did, the children of Israel would've been doomed. To go a step further, what if Jesus had refused to come and die for us? Where would you and I be today? The truth is that God places us where we are for a very specific reason. We each have a call, and as we say yes to God, the world is changed for the better, because we're each moving in the spirit, allowing the Holy Spirit to work through us for the good of the kingdom of God.

What would happen if God showed us how many people suffer and die because you and I fail to move in obedience? The point is that God is going to hold us accountable for the lives we could have, but chose not, to save. If you get nothing else from reading this book, I hope you will learn from my mistake.

II
THE WAYS GOD WORKS

I will never forget the day when a strange man came to my family's house and said he wanted to accept Jesus Christ. My dad prayed for him to become born again. The man said that he was a magician and had what he called a third eye that was located behind his head. My father spent hours casting out demons from this so-called magician and spoke blindness to his third eye. Even after that, I didn't fully understand until one day when I saw him take a leaf from a tree and rub it in his hands, and the leaf became a Haitian dollar bill, which in Haiti is called 5 gourdes. He said: "Do not tell anyone about this." I didn't tell my parents, but I did tell my friends. I was surprised to learn that I wasn't the first to see him do that. He did it in front of my friends and told them the very same thing.

It wasn't long before we realized that the man had no desire to accept Christ, but had come only to destroy. A few Christians had their own small businesses in the area, but for some reason their businesses were losing money. We had no clue that this man was responsible. One day one of the business people told my dad that someone was stealing his money. Everyday before he closed, he counted the money, but the next day he found leaves, paper, and candy wrappers mixed with less money than he had the night before. Each day he repeated the process, and the total was less than it should have been. He had even changed the locks, but it made no difference. After he closed, he stood watch overnight in order to see who the thief was, and though he saw nothing obvious there was still money missing in the morning. He told my dad something was not right. And his wasn't the only small business struggling with those issues.

It wasn't long before my mom came to ask if I had ever seen anything suspicious, and I told her the truth about the magician.

In reality, the man had not come to accept Jesus for salvation. He came as a spy to challenge God's power in us, but we didn't know that at the time. His goal was to destroy the people of God. He had tried many things, but the power of God was stronger. We started praying when we realized what was happening. It wasn't long before he realized that he couldn't accomplish his mission, and because of our prayers his third eye was rendered ineffective. He wasn't too happy about that. In fact, it wasn't long before he said he had to go. We gave him a deadline—he had to leave the next morning. Wearing his backpack he went out to the street, with many of us following, walking him out. As he approached the main gate, we all saw him put his left hand and foot on the ground, and his right hand and foot in the air. In a flash, he flew away like an airplane, right in front of us.

In that instant the fire of God hit him so hard that he crashed and burned in a huge, fiery explosion, and yet he didn't die. From what we heard he spent time running as if he was pursued by something, when there was no one chasing him. Six months later, he sent us a message and said that the power of God had really messed him up.

I've learned much from the story of that magician. Until that time I had always felt confused about miracles, because I had heard so many stories about the many amazing things the devil had done. Sometimes people in the church were even considered evil because of the amazing things they had done. And although my dad and others believed in miracles, others would talk about miracles as if they were all suspect, from the devil himself. They would say we must be really careful because there are false prophets, etc. You know the drill.

The day I met the magician I was more easily able to distinguish the difference between the work of God and the work of the devil. While the man told me many crazy and unbelievable stories, he would always do things to prove they were real.

As odd as it may sound, there was one thing that I learned from him. He had to give something in exchange for anything he wanted the devil to do for him. He had to cut himself and give his blood if he wanted the devil to give him money for a month. Cuts covered every inch of his body, and he was the most emaciated man I had ever seen. Every supernatural thing he did was very costly, and led him toward self-destruction though he actually called them miracles. The vows and chants he had to repeat and the price he had to pay for these things, made it clear that this was no game. I truly believe that the man knew the devil could come and kill him at any moment. He had even said that it was just a matter of time before he would die, giving his life in payment for all the devil had done for him.

The contrast was truly stunning, when I realized that, unlike the devil, God only wants our hearts. Because He loves us He only asks us to do things that are for our own good. He offers us life, not death and destruction. He gave us the blood of Jesus instead of demanding our blood. And even before Jesus came to die, He made arrangements for the blood of animals to cover sin, because He didn't want those He loved to suffer. Once I understood the distinctions I realized why God allowed me to be around such people.

The Holy Spirit showed me why something had to be given in order for the devil to give something in return; a price had to be paid in exchange for our pardon from sin. Through this experience I learned that the devil is very smart. He has no money, no gold, no silver, or anything else, but he is an expert liar and manipulator whose goal is to bring us down and deceive us with his clever tricks. In fact, he often does this by appealing to our selfish desires, offering us exactly what we think we want.

As believers we inherit the blessings of Abraham. The only reason the devil is able to give someone money is because someone else gave it to him. In the spiritual realm, He comes to people and demands that they give something in exchange for giving them something in return. Whatever he gives you wasn't really from him. Rather he stole it from someone else, and often he would steal someone's destiny and give it to another. In other words, he only plays the role of a middle man in human lives. For example: he might ask someone for $5,000 in order to give someone else $100.00. But we as human beings are so gullible that we fail to realize that the devil doesn't give—he only takes. He can only transfer our blessings to someone else he controls, who he plans to kill soon. That's why in the Bible Jesus always referred to him as a thief because he has nothing and can offer nothing but death and destruction in the end. Scripture says he comes to steal, kill, and destroy.

You may be wondering how he has the power to give our blessings away to others. Well, the Bible says that life and death are in the power of our tongues. We can only eat the fruits of what we speak; our lives are only a testimony to our words and actions. The words that come out of our mouths will produce a harvest that we will then live out. The enemy begins with a subtle evil thought, a whispered suggestion, and if that thought grows and is not rejected, it will become words that we act upon.

Matthew 15:18 puts it this way: "But the things that come out of the mouth come from the heart, and these make a man unclean."

The truth is that the devil has absolutely no power over a believer whose body is the temple of the Holy Spirit. The only power he has against us is the power we give him. We do this by allowing evil thoughts that attract and open the door to evil spirits. In the process of walking away from God, doing our own thing, we actually give away what rightfully belongs to us.

Remember, the enemy's goal is to kill, steal, and destroy. Ecclesiastes 10:7 tells us: "I have seen servants riding on horses, while rulers were walking beside them like slaves."

I really want you to understand this process, because many times God allows us to be around people like the magician to enable us to see certain things, but instead of learning from experience and the revelation of the truth, we fall into the enemy's traps and believe it was God's will for us to make such mistakes in order to learn. I'm here to tell you that evil mistakes are deadly and only suck the life out of us; they are never God's will, and are not meant to teach us a thing. Let me repeat that again. The mistakes we make are not meant to teach us anything good. It is only by grace that God causes everything to work together for our good because we love Him. (See Romans 8:28.) It is not because mistakes are meant to teach us. As human beings, we will always make mistakes, and some of them are fixable while others can cost us our very lives. And because He loves us God will always try to prevent us from going in the wrong direction.

For example: Judas sold Jesus to the Jewish leaders for thirty pieces of silver, but he made that deadly choice because he had a weakness for money. Remember the Jewish leaders had tried to arrest and kill Jesus many times before, but he either disappeared or he walked away right before their eyes. Judas witnessed all of that. So when he needed money he realized he could sell his insider information to the evil Jewish leaders who would never capture Jesus any other way. I find it interesting that he only asked for thirty pieces of silver, a paltry sum for such a remarkable favor. I believe that if Judas had really wanted to sell Jesus, he could've asked for a far greater sum of money, even gold. The truth is, it wasn't Judas' idea; it came from the enemy. His mistake, however, was not fixable. Now, if you really believe that our mistakes are meant to teach us, what did Judas learn from that one?

Let me repeat this point again: sin and mistakes are not meant to teach us. Matthew 5:48 tells us: "You therefore must be perfect, as your heavenly Father is perfect." If we are following the example of someone who is perfect, we will not strive with mistakes and foolish decisions every day of our lives; instead we will walk in righteousness, reckoning ourselves dead to sin, and living in obedience to the Holy Spirit. At that point we will dwell in the secret place of God instead of merely doing our own thing and succumbing to the devious tricks of the enemy.

The past cannot determine the future unless we allow it to. In another words no one can predict where I'm going because of who I've been. If that was the case, many of us would have no future at all. If only we could learn from the past and from the mistakes of others, many things would be different in our lives. We already know that as believers there is no such thing as coincidence. It's only a matter of understanding the real reason why something is happening.

III
ONE DESTINY IS SET WITH GOD

The most significant and potentially traumatic event to ever happen to my family and me was actually meant to destroy our bloodline. At the time it seemed as if God was no longer working on our behalf. It felt like we were cursed, and God had decided to punish us and get rid of our family line. At that time others were going through similar situations, but certainly not to the same extent. If I were to explain it in detail, it would fill the whole book. So I will tell it from my point of view just to help you to understand how God allows the worst things in our lives only to help us become the best we can be. Remember--don't flippantly say and believe that everything happens for a reason. Always make sure you discover that reason because until you do everything will continue to happen for the very reason you're unaware of.

I will never forget the day--December 17, 2001, the day that my life would've been snatched away if it hadn't been for God's amazing grace.

On December 16, we were informed that some dangerous men were coming to my dad's house because he disagreed with their politics. That wasn't the first time they had come to attack us, but by God's grace, and because those around us protected us, nothing had ever happened to us before that day. Once we heard they were coming we notified the neighborhood, and we all believed that it would be like other times when they had come to cast stones in opposition to us, or used firearms to shoot at everything around our house. On other occasions people have been injured, but no one ever died. We usually resisted them and refused to let them on my dad's property.

As usually happened everyone on our side who heard the news came to support us. I was on the front porch around eight in the morning playing my guitar, and I said to my little brother that I was going to see my friend who lived nearby. I didn't tell my mom where I was going because I knew she wouldn't let me go amid the chaos. As I was getting ready to leave, I looked through my window and saw a car rush into the front yard and shortly, two security guys were talking to my dad, when he suddenly got in the car and left. I thought perhaps he went to a meeting and would return shortly.

On my way to the door I could see my mom leaving, and I thought she might be going shopping and would also return soon. For some reason, I hadn't seen my older brother or my little sister anywhere, but I assumed they were somewhere nearby. My little brother and I headed to my friend's house but he wasn't there, so we returned home thinking Mom would worry, because she didn't know where we were. On my way back, we met one of my uncles, and he said, "Jean, please come with me." I refused using the excuse that my mother didn't know our whereabouts, and we had to get home. He asked us to trust him and to go with him. Once again I refused and walked away, but his next statement stopped me in my tracks. He said he didn't want to tell me, but the men who came to my house had stopped by my dad's friend's house and burned it down. He added that they also found his security guard and burned him, too.

He didn't know if others had died in the attack, but he did know that they were coming for my family, too, and the last he had heard they were ordered to shoot and burn everyone, especially the children (meaning myself and my brother).

I wondered if that was why my parents had left the house without us. I knew they would only do that if they knew something like that was about to happen. That's when it all became clear to me. I asked my uncle about my little sister and my older brother, and he said my little brother and I were the only ones missing. Apparently our parents couldn't tell anyone where they were going because there were spies in our house who made sure everyone was there during the attack. At that instant, I was terrified. I said nothing but followed my uncle to his house. But just as he said he didn't think we would be safe there we heard gunshots, and saw flames of fire going upward. He said we had to run so we left, but we couldn't go far because the area had already been secured by our enemies. My uncle took us to a friend's house, and we stayed there all day. We could hear people running as continuous gunshots filled the air, because they knew we were hiding somewhere in the area and they were hunting for us.

That afternoon, the friend whose house I had gone to earlier, arrived at the place where I was hiding. He had no idea that I was there. I gave him a phone number in order to call a friend of my parents to ask if my mom was there. When he went to call he forgot the number and actually called the wrong number not knowing I had given him the wrong number in the first place. But by the grace of God the wrong number he called was the exact number of the place where my mom was. That's how they learned we were still alive, and after dark that night she sent some cars to come and get us.

When we arrived I saw my older brother and my little sister were there too, and I praised God for that. I was asking around, whether anyone had heard anything, but no one had heard anything yet. After three days, a security man, from our house came to the place we were staying. He had been running for days and nights until he finally found us. Then he explained what little he had seen, and how God had saved his life. He said they even shot the dogs they found at the house and burned a cat alive, and only the walls of our former home remained. They burned the school and the church, as well as a building my dad used, to house those who had no place to stay. They had done it so that we would have no place to stay.

They spread the word that they would not stop searching for us until our family was dead. When we heard that we decided we had no other option but to move to another state that was far away from our former home. Our pursuers grew very upset when they learned who had hidden us, and but for the grace of God, they would've been severely punished.

Unfortunately, my older sister who was already away at university heard the news from another student because we had no way to contact her during that time. When she heard that we had burned with the house she literally went crazy to the point that when we saw her again she didn't recognize any of us. She couldn't remember my name or those of anyone else. I'm talking about a very bright young lady and talented singer, in her second year of college. While she was in that condition I played my guitar and we sang every song she knew and loved, until one day by grace she became her old self again.

When we left the state, we felt like it was over. We assumed that we could leave our lives and no one would bother us afterward, but we were wrong. The hunt for us was so intense that we even had to leave the place where we had fled. But in the next place, we stayed isolated, contacting no one until God opened the door to go to the United States.

At that point it felt as if we were cursed, because though others had been in trouble, they had been able to resume their normal lives, while we could not. The life of luxury we had previously known was a thing of the past, but at that point God could really teach us, because we had no choice but to depend on Him for everything. We arrived with nothing but the clothes on our backs and had no money whatsoever. In reality, we had to start over and learn how to do everything on our own, depending on God for the rest.

A friend of ours was kind enough to allow my mom and her five children to stay with them. My father found the transition much too hard, and ended up leaving the country for another place with a similar culture to the one we left behind. You can imagine what it was like for a woman and her five children to live with a family of eight in a four-bedroom house. Remember, we had been living like royalty, and suddenly everything changed. We had no idea how to manage on our own. I had no idea how to wash my clothes, or to wash dishes. One small step at a time I had to learn how to survive. I thank God for the wonderful friends who took us in.

Most of the people who used to stand with my dad regarding his politics turned away from him so that he didn't hear from them at all after awhile. They apparently thought we were cursed or would bring them back luck. Sometimes news would get back to us that they were making great progress in their lives, and the truth is that we were hurt. Those times only confirmed what we already knew. Because human beings are fickle, we must not count on them the way we count on Jesus, the only one who truly cares for us. Since that time I learned to mentally put my friends in different categories, after deciding that friends are much like shoes. Once a person grows, no matter how nice his shoes are, they will not fit anymore, and if he forces his feet into them, he will be miserable. At the same time, true friends, the ones we only discover during times of trial, come through when others leave. The best category of friends has only one member, a very rare one, who will be faithful forever. His name is Jesus.

I said that He is a rare friend because I've learned that He is the one who always seeks to help us when we are in need. He continually tries to get close to us. And though He is, in reality, our only alternative we often go to Him only as a last resort, when we have no other options.

It took us awhile before we could see things from a different perspective. Our dream was to return to Haiti, but the one who brought us here had much better plans for us.

After about seven months, my mom decided to move out of her friend's house and live on her own with her five children ranging in age from seven to twenty. None of us were working and we had no income. The pastor of the church we attended was quite interested in our talent because my sister could really sing, and my brother and I are also musically gifted. So the pastor decided to help my mom get a place that was closer to the church. I can't tell you how God did it because none of us had Social Security at the time, or even a bank account, or anything that is usually required to rent a single family house, but by grace the Lord helped us to secure the place.

When we moved to the house we had nothing but a radio and one CD entitled, "God is Faithful," that was in French. It was given to us by a stranger who came to visit my mom's friend from France. Basically, we had no choice, but to trust God because we had no money coming in, or help from anyone we knew. So, we would listen to the songs from that CD over and over again. We had no car, and no one nearby to whom we could go for help. In fact, as a family, we were alone together 24/7, except when we went to church, when we could get a ride. Some days, all we could do was cry, but somehow we knew that God would make a way. I remember one day my sister approached my mom, and it was that time of the month, but we had no money to purchase the supplies she needed. My mom cried like a baby, and soon we all cried, until someone finally turned on the CD.

The words of the song said: "God is faithful; He will never change. He is my Lord, my Rock, and my Peace." You may not believe this, but I can promise you that if God hadn't taken us down that path, I wouldn't be serving Him today.

I often recalled the days in Haiti when I had everything and still thought I needed more, when I now had nothing. As you can imagine I cherished the fact that I was even alive after nearly losing my life. Those moments helped me to understand the real value of life. I've also learned to appreciate whatever I'm blessed with, though I no longer get attached to material things. The truth is that I didn't know how good I had it until everything was gone. At that time there I failed to understand that God is in control. Now, I'm happy that I went through it because those struggles have made me the person God wants me to be today.

I can honestly say that apart from this experience, I wouldn't be a man that God could count on. I have always had great plans for life. For as long as I can recall, I wanted God to do things for me, but He could not count on me to live only for Him. I wanted Him to help me be the person *I* wanted to be, to fulfill *my* dreams and desires. I had plans that included churches, but only according to my own agenda. I wanted to do things in ways that pleased me. Consider this: we are born into this world to fulfill a written prophecy. God already has a plan and purpose for every day, month, and year of our lives. He will not erase what's already been written merely to satisfy our selfish desires.

The reality I want you to understand is this: God doesn't care as much about making us rich and happy as making us holy, able to reflect the glory of God, and live out our destiny to win the world for Christ. Look at it this way: without you, your possessions mean nothing. It takes you to have what you have, and what you have will always be attracted to you exclusively because of your uniqueness. So, why should I be worried when I know that I'm supposed to be the golden prince who can and will always make things happen by the grace of God if I walk in His Spirit?

Across the street lived a man we didn't know and had never met, who one day came to our house and told something remarkable: God had laid it on his heart to support us financially. He was a stranger who didn't know any of us, and yet God had placed on his heart to do this incredible thing. He gave my mom a check for the first month and enough money to pay for utilities. Remember I told you that none of us had work, though it wasn't because we didn't want to work. We came to the U.S.

for political asylum, and we were in process of getting our residency papers. So every month, we would receive a check from him, and he never missed a payment nor was he ever late. God used this man to bless us and we were incredibly grateful.

A few years later, we decided to move from Florida to North Carolina for schooling purposes. When Mom went and informed our benefactor he offered to drive us there. I praise God for this wonderful man and his family who supported our family for exactly seven years—truly a gift from God.

A few weeks after our arrival, I signed up to go to school and got a job working nights at the Holiday inn, in Asheville as part of the set-up crew. I was the only black person on the crew; everyone else was Spanish-speaking, and our supervisor was from Brazil. For some reason most of them, including my supervisor, disliked me. Late at night, everyone would be sitting somewhere, and I alone would have a long list of things to do. I wasn't happy about it, but I had no choice if I wanted the work. I would always smile at them as if I were ignorant of their evil treatment, but in my mind, I told myself to keep working and going to school, because the same God who brought me that far knew everything, and He would make a way. My supervisor would mistreat me every day, and sometimes when things were too much for me, I went and told his boss. As a result he got really upset with me, and for no other reason than that he often sent me home.

So, I decided to say nothing, and do both their jobs and my own, knowing that things would not stay like that forever. After a few months, my supervisor's boss called me into his office and told me that he had a supervisor who needed someone to work with him mornings, but he preferred a black person since he himself was black (North Carolina is a very racially-segregated state). So, I was transferred to the morning crew, and my new supervisor was very nice to me. At that point I began to understand the work of God in my life. At that time, I thought that was it, but God had much more in store for me. My supervisor said that he had been working with them for thirteen years. As a black person, his method of protecting his job was to never train anyone, but because he liked me, he offered to train me.

After I was familiar and comfortable in every aspect of the job, he trusted me so much that he began to relax and allowed me to do his job. A few weeks later, something happened between him and his boss, so he was let go. His boss called me into the office again and asked me if I could do the job. When I said that I believed I could he said I had the job. The Brazilian who had been my night supervisor had left the job long before I became a morning supervisor because he'd found another job. For some reason that job wasn't working out for him, so he came back. My boss told him that he no longer had a supervisory position for him, but we needed a guy in the morning crew, and if he was willing he could work under my supervision.

He needed a job, so he had no choice but to take the job. When the news came to me, I started to think with pride, and I only had one thing in mind-- sweet vengeance. The very first day when he showed up for work, I made him work like a slave and didn't allow him to take a lunch break, but at the same time something inside told me not to do it. When I went home that day, my conscience was killing me. I wasn't happy with God because I knew He was responsible for my feelings of guilt. I had big plans for this guy, but I was getting soft. So, the next day, when he started to call me boss, and was very flexible and obedient I was touched by the way he was acting.

I said, "Do you remember what you used to do to me?" He said. "Yes, I do." I asked him, "What have I ever done to you to deserve that kind of treatment? What do you expect me to do right now?"

He said, "I'm really sorry, and I don't expect anything from you. Please just don't fire me." I told him, "I will not fire you, nor will I treat you the way you treated me." As a result we became good friends and worked together for nearly two years until I left North Carolina.

At that time I wasn't really living for God, but His favor was with me, and because of that grace I was drawing closer to Him without realizing it. In a way, He was in the process of forming my character. There was a side of me that I've never known before that was developing, and I was becoming wiser little by little because of His presence in my life.

I want you to understand something. Whether we believe it or not, God's way is and will always be fair. Do you know that God would not have given me that position if He had known I was going to treat the man the same way he treated me? The difference between us and those who are in the world is very simple. It's called actions. Unbelievers should never be able to do what we do. And we should never allow ourselves to sink low enough to mimic their evil ways.

Jesus said we are to love our neighbors as we love ourselves. When we refuse to treat others the way we want them to treat us God has no choice but to take us back and let us go through the same process over and over until we've learned that little lesson. So next time our neighbor gets in that situation, we will definitely know how he is feeling no matter what kind of person he is. We will treat him like we would want to be treated because love is unconditional. A wise man will learn to empathize with the pain of others without actually going through it because that way, tough situations will not have to be his teacher.

Consider this: there are no defeats for the righteous. We must consider defeats as stepping stones that build our muscles for future challenges. That's why we must not worry about what others do to us; God will turn everything around for our good. They only help us to become stronger and wiser.

Take students for instance. It's not easy for them to wake up early and go to school every day. Sometimes they feel tempted to quit, but good parents won't allow them to do that.

And just like certain students some people repeat the same classes over and over again and never learn the lessons they are supposed to learn. Now they may get away with that on earth, but God will never give a diploma or a degree to someone who hasn't mastered the subject matter. In fact, there is no skipping in God's classes. Remember what we read earlier in Hosea 4:6? The people of God perish due to lack of knowledge.

IV
DESTINY

What is Destiny?

Destiny is a vocation, or fate, or a fortune . . . something special that distinguishes each one of us from all others. One person's destiny is unique from those of others. One can try to imitate many great people and do everything they did, but it will be a hollow victory. That's because it won't be the right destiny if it's not God's customized and perfect will for us as individuals. Only something uniquely ours allows us to rise to a higher place where everyone can see Christ in us moving in the spirit.

To a certain degree we all tend to imitate others, because we do what we have seen. Often times when we do or say something we become the reflection of the person we imitate, whether we realize it or not. Many people imitate someone who did something great because they believe that will make them great, but there is one thing missing from that equation. Without a special additive, that includes a combination of both personality and uniqueness one can never be distinctive. Jesus is the role model for all of us. He is looking for those who will follow His steps to become exactly what He intended, rather than a poor replica of someone else. As our model, He sets a plan and purpose for every single one of us. As we follow Him through the power of the Holy Spirit He will guide us toward our destiny.

WHO SAYS YOUR FUTURE DICTATES ON YOUR PAST?

For example: God blessed Abraham abundantly because of the unique step he took to believe God, leave his homeland and move to a far distant place where God told him to go. That's why he is called the "Father of faith." And one of the reasons we inherit the blessings of God today is because of his obedience.

Moses could have chosen to live happily for the rest of his life in the palace of an Egyptian king, but instead he chose to lead a stubborn nation through a desert. He is one of the greatest godly leaders who ever lived.

Job didn't deserve what he went through, but amid his personal tragedy he chose to praise God, who, in the end, blessed him with more than he could ever have imagined.

David was a sinner, but he never ran away from God no matter how he badly had sinned. Instead he ran to God, who called him a man after His own heart.

God offered Solomon anything his heart could desire, but with all those things to choose from the only thing he asked for was wisdom. Scripture calls Solomon the wisest man who ever lived. And as a result God blessed him with riches as well.

Jesus was the only man who was ever required to die for sins He would never commit. He took our place and died as our substitute, paying the price so we could go free. God gave Him a name above all names. In fact, no one can go to God without going through Jesus.

I could go on and on listing those in the Bible who made it to a higher place. The only thing required of them was to follow their destinies and allow their uniqueness to show and become vessels the Holy Spirit could pour through.

But that honor wasn't reserved for them alone. It is for anyone who is willing to be himself and show his uniqueness, submitting to God. Believe it or not, the unique part of us is the only thing that can move God like He moved on behalf of Abraham, Isaac, Jacob, David, Daniel, Shadrach, Meshach, and Abednego, etc....

Until we realize that we are unique we will never take the steps necessary to live out our destiny. Some time ago I realized something remarkable about God. He doesn't really take pleasure in quantity; He would rather receive a small amount from us, as long as it is of excellent quality—the best we have to offer--ourselves. We can not expect to be great if we aren't willing, in the power of the Spirit, to do something unexpected that has never been done before. And in order for that to happen we need to use the unique side of us and step out in faith. We can only expect something great to happen when we overcome our limitations.

There are 365 days in a single year: that is fifty-two weeks, twelve months. The strange thing is that none of them is alike. Each one is different from the others. The reason is that circumstances change every second we live.

The Bible says that God's mercies are new every morning—renewed on a daily basis. It happens that way because everything is moving toward something, and our needs change. What we needed to survive yesterday is very different from what we need for today and tomorrow. The person who is walking toward a destiny must use the tools God has given him on a daily basis. We cannot rely on yesterday's grace to feed our spirits today. No one can rely on what he ate yesterday to survive the next day. This is a continual process because tomorrow will always have its own needs.

God is unlimited in the number of ways He can do things. But that's exactly where many of us get stuck. We are waiting on

God to do something in a certain way, and when we don't see it we get discouraged and start doubting His promises. We don't understand that although it may be the same problem we've had before, God will use a different means to deliver us. There is never a boring, routine response from our multifaceted God. That is one way He proves His worthiness to mankind. He can do the impossible and still make it work every time.

Dwelling in Our Comfort Zone (the past)

It is vital that as believers our lives produce excellent fruit. Jesus said that a tree would be known by its fruit. So how does that apply to our comfort zones? Many people are dwelling in their comfort zones and are not even aware of it. Some even believe that they are doing great spiritually because in their eyes everything looks stable and peaceful. From that vantage point spiritual growth may seem unnecessary. But believe it or not, growth is essential. In fact, I can say unequivocally that we are either growing spiritually or dying spiritually.

Those who dwell in their comfort zones always believe that God will take them somewhere higher, but the truth is that they will never do anything different from what they have always done if they stay where they are. They forget that God is always moving, and His ways are not repetitious. If the move of God remains the same in someone's life, it is because there has been no progress—no growth in that person's life. He is stuck in a particular period of time and place that is boring, annoying, and meaningless. If you were to play a CD and the song kept repeating or it gets stuck there, you would check that CD to discover where it is damaged. Ask the Holy Spirit to help you realize where and why you are stuck. In this case ignorance is not bliss; it can be very destructive.

How do you expect to get to your destiny when everything you do is repetitious? There is no way that a person will get anywhere when he is dwelling in his comfort zone. Action must be taken. Perhaps you've heard the saying: Insanity is defined as repeating the same behaviors expecting different results.

Where Does Our Desire Originate?

A man once told me a story that opened my eyes to many things. The story goes like this: Once upon a time there were three little trees that believed in God, and they were sharing their dreams with each other.

The first tree said: "God knows my heart and He knows what I desire the most. My desire is to become a big, strong box that carries gold, diamonds, precious stones for a king."

The second one said: "That is nothing compared to what I have in mind. I know God will fulfill my desire. I will become a big ship, but not just any ship--one that will only carry kings."

The third one said: "You guys ask for too much. The only thing I want is to be taller than any other tree, and then I want to grow as high as heaven and spend time with God. That's all I want from Him."

After they shared their dreams, they waited in the forest for their destinies to be fulfilled. Many seasons passed, but they held on to their faith because they believed that God would fulfill their desires. One day, some people came around and cut down the first tree. As they were carrying it away the tree looked back at the other trees wearing a hopeless look. Clearly these people didn't look like the kind who would cut down a tree for a king.

As it disappeared through the forest, the other two were praying that God would fulfill their destinies because they didn't want to end up like their friend. The men took the first tree and fashioned it into three little boxes and sold them to some men who were traveling to Bethlehem. When the other trees heard the news they felt sad because they couldn't understand why God had let that happen to their friend. It made them unsure that God had their best interests in mind. They believed that the enemy took their friend and God had nothing to stop it.

The others were praying hard when some men came and cut down the second tree, and as they were carrying it away, it was thinking that this was the end, because its dreams would never come true. It wondered if maybe God didn't really hear or care how they felt, or perhaps He did it on purpose for His own selfish reasons.

They cut the tree into little pieces and sold them to a fisherman who used them to build a small boat because that's all he could afford. Although the fisherman was a good man and let other people ride in his boat, that wasn't the dream the little tree had in mind. The little tree thought his life was over because a king would never want to ride in him, even if he was drowning.

The news spread quickly to the last first and last tree. They both wept because they believed it was the work of the devil hindering their destiny. The first one sent a message to the last one to pray harder so that he would grow up to the heavens. At the end of the message he added, "When you see God, tell Him we're sorry that we were so self-centered. Tell Him not to forget us in the next world. It wasn't His fault that we didn't live out our dreams."

As the last tree heard what his friend said the same men returned to cut him down. The tree screamed with a loud voice, "God, please don't allow them to cut me down, because I will never grow tall enough to grow close to reach heaven."

It seemed as if no one had listened to its sad story. The men cut it into two posts and made a cross on which to hang someone. The last tree thought: *It's over for me—now I will never fulfill my dream. Why did God allow me to have that kind of dream all my life? Just look at me. Why me, Lord? Why me?*

While the three of them were grieving over their lost dreams, God appeared and said to the first one: "What is it, my child?" He burst into tears and said, "Why didn't you listen to us when we called? Now, it is too late." God said, "The desire you had to carry diamonds and gold was for kings. Do you know where that desire came from?" Before the tree could reply, God said, "I put that desire in you for My glory. Do you remember the three men who bought you before you were made into three boxes? Did you know that when they went to Bethlehem, the little child they went to visit was the King of kings, and you were the one to carry those gifts to Him? Your destiny was to carry gold and diamonds not just for any old king, but for the very King of all kings!"

God said to the next tree: "A king came to earth and crossed the Jordan River on you many times. He stood on top of you and taught many people the Word of God. You were supposed to carry kings, and not only did you carry a king, but you carried the King of kings."

God said to the third tree: "Do you know that among all the trees you were designed to hold the King of kings? You wanted to be close to Me, but I gave you something better. I was crucified on you. We spent many long hours together on Calvary, and no one will ever forget My cross."

After God spoke to them like that, they all felt deep regret realizing they had misunderstood what was happening when God was actually fulfilling their deepest desires. At that point they understood that God had actually listened and fulfilled their destinies.

God continued: "Remember that you were all created for My purpose and My glory. Every good gift comes from Me. Your desires actually originate in My imagination, and I will always do what I say, but in My way and for My glory."

Who are we to tell God how and when to do things? It is only by grace that He allows us to know what He wants to do and where He is taking us. But it is not for us to choose how it is going to be done. If the desire comes from God, He has a specific way of accomplishing it. Our job is to keep the vision alive and believe He will do what He promised.

The Chosen Ones

When you have been called by God, you have the choice to accept or reject the calling. Remember, it took me nearly ten years before I accepted the call of God upon my life. Keep in mind that just accepting a calling doesn't make you a chosen one. When I accepted His calling it didn't mean I was qualified to be one of His chosen ones. Matthew 22:14 tells us: "For many people are invited, but few are chosen."

Chosen means to be especially selected, based on one's quali-
fications. A king would not send someone to represent him if that
person didn't think like the king. A representative of a king is a
carbon copy of the king in his thinking and opinions. In order to
represent a king there are rules to learn and preparations to
make such as: classes, tests, and trials that will prove that one is
worthy to be chosen. It is much the same way in the kingdom of
God, where certain things happen in order to build our faith, to
train, and to prepare us for a specific mission or field.

When God takes us out of our comfort zones, He will mold us,
purify us, and squeeze us in order to conform us into the image of
Christ, so we clearly reflect His character. This process is also
known as a trial or a test. Great value comes with being purified
and transformed from what we used to be. These are the qualities
that make us valuable to the kingdom of God. He will always take
us out of our comfort zones, because we cannot grow and mature
there. And while a comfort zone is obviously the most comfortable place to be, we cannot stay there indefinitely if we want to live
out our destiny. In order to be useful to the kingdom we must
spend time in the desert, where we undergo testing that matures
us. And while it's never easy in the desert we must go there in
order to be able to minister to the needs of others. The harsh
truth is that we cannot be of service apart from the desert
experience. Some believers have no intention of leaving their
comfort zone for any reason, but if that's the case they will never
fulfill the destiny they were designed for.

In every trial or tribulation there are lessons that must be
learned. Many of us go through struggles in our lives, but seem
unable to get through them because we never learn the lessons
that accompany the situation. Learning the lesson is actually the

solution to our situation. It's like God places us there to find a key, and that key will unlock the exit door to escape our trials. Thinking back I can identify every trial that never ended until I learned the lesson God wanted me to learn. 1 Thessalonians 2:4 tells us: "It was God who gave us this work but only after he **tested** us and saw that we could be trusted to do it." He will always allow us to go through the wilderness, and there we must obtain the key in order to get out.

I've been in church all my life and never missed a service. I felt like I was doing okay, until the Holy Spirit made me see things from a different point of view. The only way for Him to do that was to send a trial. That's what I want you to understand. If you fail to learn the lesson and find the key, you will remain in a state of misery for a very long time. James 1:2-3 tells us: "Consider it pure joy, my brothers, whenever you face trials of many kinds, because you know that the *testing* of your faith develops perseverance."

Why Can't God Just Do Things for Us?
Why Do We Have to Suffer?

As human beings we try to take care of ourselves, doing our best to stay healthy, but the things we do toward that end may sometimes be difficult. The medicine we take to recover or maintain our good health may not taste good. Our daily exercise may not be easy, but we go through it because we know it is good for us. We know that one day we will reap the benefits we for which we worked so hard.

God's intention is not for anyone to suffer or to perish, but because of our old nature we seldom appreciate things that cost us nothing. In the Old Testament God attempted to save mankind through the use of animal sacrifice, but we rejected that offer. A major sacrifice had to take place using God's Son Himself, and we have to be continually reminded of the cost of that sacrifice in order for us to understand and give it the value it deserves.

We tend to make light of anything that comes easy in life because of our nature. Even if we want to, we cannot muster respect for anything that takes no effort. Those with the greatest appreciation for life are usually the ones who have endured the most heartache. The best rest one ever finds always comes after an exhausting day. Foods usually taste better after a long period of time without eating. We all know that water has no taste, but a cup of cold water tastes amazing to a very thirsty soul.

Remember that God uses this method to keep us balanced and give us His perspective.

The only way we will ever understand why certain things happen, is to let Him take us to the next level where we can see things more clearly. You may wonder: what's so important about going higher? Every time we find that we're able to understand things we've never understood before, we have grown to a higher level and become spiritually wiser as well, in the power of the Holy Spirit. The thing is that once we reach the next level, there will be more challenges, but at an even higher level, and for us to conquer that level will require a great deal of patience and determination because it is hard to discern the moment when we change levels. In fact, you may have times when you think you used to be smarter or have a better understanding of things, and now you've lost your edge. You feel that your spiritual life is going backward instead of forward. All these thoughts can come into your head. But the truth is that you don't understand things at that level because they are higher and it requires more effort to spiritually discern them in that place. And the process requires times of deep soaking in God's presence to attain it.

It is much like the process of lifting weights. After bench-pressing 200 lbs. ten times a lifter decides to go up to 250 lbs. though it may not possible to do ten repetitions that day. The truth is that it requires intense training in order to be able to get where you want to go.

The Right Field

Now, let's say I'm a soccer player. My training has nothing to do with hand dribbling or shooting a basket ball. In order to become a soccer player, there are specific classes, practices, and training sessions required in order to play the game.

It is the same for a Christian. In order to become a chosen one, one has to know the field that he or she had been called into, and what training is required for that sport. The danger of not being prepared is that the player will face injury and suffering, because he is ill-equipped to play. Let me explain.

Soccer players become very comfortable using their feet in the field, but if you tell them to use hands instead of feet, they will be uncomfortable and will have the tendency to kick the ball because their mind was trained to kick rather than hand dribble. The same is true for Christians, who must be equipped for the field where God called them to play. If we are in the wrong field, life will be difficult because we are not equipped for the obstacles we will be face there.

On the other hand we can be in right field and still not be in the right position. According to Ephesians 4:11-13 there is

the five-fold ministry that includes: Apostle, Prophet, Evangelist, Pastor, and Teacher. That is for the leaders. For everyone
else, though the positions differ, the same principle applies.
We must be in just the right position to in order to receive the
blessings.

Now, you may have wondered how you can know where
you are supposed to be. The way we can understand our
calling is very simple.

Every born again Christian has been given at least one gift
(see Romans 12:6; 1 Peter 4:10) given according to God's grace.
In order for us to be trained in our gifts, God will place us in a
specific situation that will enable us to grow in that gift. A gift is
just like a magnet; it attracts problems. Much like doctors, who
treat illness, if they've done it for a while they've seen every kind
of health problem. Basically, asking for a gift is like asking for
problems.

Sometimes, people around us spot the gifts in us while we are
struggling to know our calling. If those close to me often call me
for one specific reason that they need help with, then I must have
something extra to offer that others don't have. A gift is the thing
given by the Holy Spirit over and above a normal level of human
skill or training. The only way for the gifted one to recognize the
gift in himself, is through the observations of others. In the same
way that I can't see my face without a mirror, I can't experience
my own gift without the help of others. You only know it's there
when it impacts the lives of others.

From my brief description you probably realize it's impossible to discover the answer if you sit at home wondering. So, if
you really want that gifting in the area of your call, just start
with the basics which is to pray and seek God, then go and

encourage others. Then watch to see what kind of feedback you get from them.

In the same way that Jesus Christ is the gift from God to humanity, those who receive such gifts bless the kingdom of God. In conclusion, your gift is a continuous source of light that will make a way for you in times of darkness, when problems arise, and when you face challenges.

V
THE BEGINNING OF MY SPIRITUAL

There were many things that happened throughout my journey, but the one that I really want to share is how I got to where I am now. Please fasten your seatbelt as I walk you through it, and hold on for a wild ride.

My parents are very strict when it comes to church and school. Even today, when it's church time, my mom demands that those who live under her roof attend services whether they like it or not. I used to go to church because I had no choice, and sometimes I enjoyed playing a little piano while I was there. And while I loved playing piano or keyboard in church, most of the time church was so boring that I often asked myself: *do they really know what they are doing?* That's one of the reasons why I didn't like church.

Now, you might think after having that kind of dramatic experience with God, I would automatically be on fire for Him. But the truth is that my fire didn't last long. The devil saw where God wanted to use me, and realized that my attitude wasn't quite good enough to keep up the momentum. I was called at age fifteen, but by the age of twenty-four I still hadn't made up my mind to follow Christ. And though I didn't realize it at the time, I had made a choice not to serve God when I refused to make that choice. In other words, living for myself was, in reality, living for the enemy.

To be perfectly honest my life was up and down with God. It wasn't because I didn't want to be a godly man, or I didn't know what to do. I knew the way and knew what to do, but couldn't do it and make it stick. I did what many other Christians do whenever I heard something that touched me. I merely reacted out of emotion. Years went by, and while I was growing older physically, I had never grown past the spiritual age of fifteen.

I often used to hang out with my little brother and others who were my best friends at the time. We were all very close; we played basketball, soccer, and also played music together.

We used to be in church, when the pastor, who was talking to the people, would ask us to play something in the background, and we would play *Fifty Cents*, *Nelly* and other songs so popular in the world at the time. Picture this: While everyone was praying, we played worldly songs in the background. We would spend time listening to songs and learning them during the week so we could go and play them at church on Sunday.

That was my lifestyle, people, and I didn't want anyone to judge me for it. I thought I was doing alright. One thing I forgot was that every tree is judged by its fruit. My actions and fruit said it all for me. Whenever I would pick up a Bible and read something I thought I was spiritual again. I had the wrong concept of God. I can't speak for anyone else who was with me, but I can speak for myself. 1 John 2:15 says: "Do not love the world or anything in the world. If anyone loves the world, the love of the Father is not in him." I don't know about you, but I've loved some things that were not bad in and of themselves, but they were evidence of the rebellious condition of my heart.

I can tell you this because at the time I was on the other side of this issue. To unbelievers it might seem normal to listen to whatever you want or even to do what you want. Let's be honest. In reality, if I say I'm a follower of someone but fail to follow his rules, am I really a follower at all? I hope you will honestly answer that question.

One day, I started receiving crazy texts from my brother who told us that he wanted to change his life. We had all done that from time to time, but this time, things were different; he was quite serious. He was tired of living life his own way and wanted to follow Jesus. At first I took it as a joke although I knew he wasn't joking. I told him that I was with him in his decision, but I didn't mean a word of it. I only said that to shut him up.

At that point he began to distance himself from us, and it wasn't long before my fiancé, who was also a close friend, decided that she, too, wanted to change her life. On hang-out night, I would severely miss my two closest friends. Sometimes, I tried to have fun, but deep down inside I couldn't because I started to feel that I, too, needed to do something else with my life. One day I really felt tired of my lifestyle, and I said to the Lord, "I want to change my life. I know You've called me, but I was young and stupid back then. Now, I need you to help me to make the right decision." It wasn't easy for me because I didn't know how or where to start. I had absolutely no idea how to change my life. I'd been in church all my life and I thought I'd seen it all, but my fiancé and my brother seemed to have something that I'd never seen before, and from what I could see they were over the top with zeal. I missed my fiancé and my brother, but I refused to follow the path they had chosen because I never follow anything I don't understand.

In a very prideful way I argued that I was my own person, with no need to follow others. As my pride continued to grow, I began to see things the devil's way. Always remember that when we begin to think we know everything, God will sit quietly and let us do our thing without interfering, until we let go completely. During that time I developed an idea about how my brother, my fiancée, my mom, and my sister were lost, so I prayed that God would help them see the error of their ways. To be honest, they were going to church, fasting (which they'd never done before), reading the Bible (I don't think my brother even owned a Bible before), and lived to passionately reflect the love of God. I, on the other hand was doing nothing serious with my life. I went to work, came home, watched TV, and then some more TV, and hung with my friends. And I really believed that they were lost, while I was okay. Talk about being deceived . . .

Every tool that the devil used to destroy me took me one step closer to that awful destiny. Every day my mom, my little sister, and brother would have prayer at the house. The main problem I had with them was the speaking in tongues. Remember I told you that my mom used to force us to go to church? Well, now she wasn't even asking me to go with her. It's like I was in the house, but no one seemed to be aware of my existence, and they didn't seem to care if I went to church or not. It's not because they didn't talk to me. They were very nice to me, but I felt uncomfortable around them and I didn't know why. It was just very annoying to see them reading and praying all the time, especially when I couldn't understand what they said.

My friends and I jokingly agreed that we would have believed if it was one of us speaking in tongues, but there was no way we'd believe them. We forgot that my brother was once one of us.

The idea of going to the church where my family was going grew stronger daily, but again my main concern was about the praying in tongues. So one day, I decided to find out for myself about the tongues thing. I prayed and said I would go that church tonight, if He would make me speak in tongues as a sign that it was real. I promised to follow Him for the rest of my days if it was real, but if it didn't happen I would know it wasn't real. And if it wasn't real I asked Him to open my family's eyes and show them that they'd gotten lost and confused along the way and to bring them back to reality. I believed that their intentions were good, but they were doing the wrong thing.

Even as I said those words deep down inside I knew I was the one who was lost. I just had no control over my life. I knew I wasn't serving God the way I should've, and I knew my family was serving God better than I was, but the devil was using me to tear down their faith. Though I believed God was real and with Him anything was possible, I didn't believe He would answer.

Even if that tongues thing was real, I knew that I wasn't good enough for God to listen to me or to do what I asked. That afternoon I got up and went to the service to see what would happen. When I got there, everything went normally until they were praying, and at that point I closed my eyes and reminded God of my challenge.

During the service nothing convincing happened to me, so I wasn't happy. After service, I didn't say a word to anyone, I just got up, got in my car and left. As I was driving, I was praying in a rage. I was praying in a way that I had never prayed before. I was very loud—screaming and yelling. Spit came out of my mouth when I said, "God I know that You called me, and I've never forgotten that. I know I'm not doing Your will right now, but at least save my family from this false doctrine. They have the desire to serve you. I told you I was ready to follow you if you made me speak in tongues, but since it is didn't happen, it must not be from you. If you are the one who spoke to me that night, show yourself again, and save my family, please!" As I was shouting those words, I began to lose control of the car and of my trashy mouth. In the next instant something came over me, and while I was conscious, but I wasn't the one driving anymore. The power was so strong that I couldn't bear it on my body. I was aware of my existence, but I wasn't me anymore.

I had no idea what was happening. My first thought was that maybe God was mad at me and trying to kill me. After a few seconds I was overcome by peace. That's when my mouth started to speak in a different language, and I had no control over that—as if it was doing it without my consent. If you've never experienced the gift of tongues, let me tell you that it's a beautiful thing. I felt a peace deep within that I had never experienced in my entire life—as if all my worries, troubles, and sins had simply disappeared.

In the Bible Jesus said, "Come unto me, and I will give you rest." Someone can fix your car and save you from a break down. Someone else can help you pay the bill and save you a great sum of money. But who can stop your mind from wandering? Who can fill up the gaps inside of you? Sometimes, we live with a wrong belief for so long that we are convinced it's true. We can even tell ourselves that it is in the will of God. But I can tell you the difference because I was on the other side. I thought I had peace until I finally experienced real peace. I had settled for less that God's best when I could've had so much more.

During that experience I couldn't control my mouth, but in my heart I said, "God, you've won my heart—you've got another warrior. I've seen plenty of amazing things happen since You called me. I know You orchestrated everything that's happened in my life. From this moment on, I will do whatever You want me to do. I'm Yours forever. I know it will be hard, but if You keep talking to me the way You did tonight, I will never stray." John 10:3 &5 says, "The watchman opens the gate for him, and the sheep listen to his voice. He calls his own sheep by name and leads them out. When he has brought out all his own, he goes on ahead of them, and his sheep follow him because they know his voice. But they will never follow a stranger; in fact, they will run away from him because they do not recognize a stranger's voice."

When I got home, my mouth was still praying independent of me so I stayed in the car waiting for it to stop. After a while, I figured it wasn't going to stop so I got out of the car and walked toward the door still praying in tongues. My brother was outside when he saw me coming, so he went and called my mom. They all came outside and were laughing at me. I still couldn't talk to them, so I went straight to my room. A while later my mouth stop praying, and trust me by that time it was so dry that I had to drink lots of water. I was anxious to call one of my friends and tell him that the praying in tongues thing was real.

That same night, I called him and I told him that something strange had just happened. As usual he joked about it, but I said, "I'm serious, man." He said, "What is it?" I explained, "You know me better than anyone else. You know that I don't fall for anything because I know where I stand. Well, that speaking in tongues thing is real, man." My friend wasn't too happy hearing that, and he said: "So now you're one of them, too." I shook my head thinking, *here we go again.* I said, "Remember we said if one of us spoke in tongues we all would believe, because we've known each other so well, and we would never do anything to harm one another?" Unfortunately he wasn't convinced, and he's since walked away from our friendship. The thing to remember is that it's not our responsibility to convince others. It's God's responsibility.

I've experienced both sides of this issue, so I feel I can offer advice in this area. Always remember that it's very hard for human beings to adapt to new things. And yet nothing is impossible for the God we serve. There are some great stories in both the Old and New Testament Scriptures, and they are very believable, until it comes time to believe those kinds of signs, wonders and miracles for our own lives. Though our spirits may be convinced that our God can do anything, our old nature hinders us from believing it is so. It's much like the concept of giving back to God. We know it in theory, but when it comes time to put it into practice, we struggle to follow through.

From the moment of my revelation I began to pray for hours every day, and dedicated myself to serving God in every possible way. My prayer times were long and late at night, because there were so many needs to cover in prayer. When I heard that someone had a problem I would continue to pray for that person daily until I knew he had his breakthrough.

I didn't know God's plan for my life, but I knew that He really had something special in mind for me. If it had been up to me, I wouldn't be where I'm now because that wasn't even on my agenda. In fact, I didn't believe that God could use me because of my areas of weakness, but I was wrong.

Along the way, I found that I actually cared about people, and wanted Him to use me to help others experience God the way I knew Him. I wanted to be an instrument to win young people who are like I was. I really wanted to be used for His glory. I was really motivated knowing He had spoken to me twice, very clearly, once when I was a teen, and again in the car. I believed that if He could do it once, He could do it again. My prayer was: *God teach me Your ways, talk to me like You did before. Let me know You're with me, and I will do Your will.*

My desire to help was so strong that I began sharing the gospel, trying to convince others that it was true, but I was basically getting nowhere. So I asked the Holy Spirit to teach me His way because I felt like I was hurting people instead of bringing them closer to God. I didn't do it intentionally, but I was offending people instead of winning them for Christ. I meant well, but because I was still an immature believer I didn't know what to say. In fact, I began to reject those who were not part of my church. Others from my church did the same thing, unintentionally offending their family and friends, instead of loving them to Christ. In spite of that I was excited to be part of my church body.

It wasn't long before I began to desire spiritual gifts so that people wouldn't be wounded by my words. All I wanted was for God to use me day and night. I didn't know that God had already answered that prayer until one day when I went to another church. I didn't plan on going because on the previous night we had an all-night prayer meeting at my mother's house before finally going to bed around four or five a.m. Before we even went to bed, we felt an urgency attend that service.

I struggled to wake up after so little sleep, but I was going because of my great desire for God. We went to the church, and the pastor didn't know any of us at all. We were visitors. He ministered the Word and spoke to a few people that Sunday, but didn't even see us. After service, I said to someone that I wanted to speak to him. I waited for a while, and finally he came to meet me. I told him that I wanted to experience the fire of God. He said, "You already have a little of that fire deep inside you. If you seek God, fast, pray, and dwell in God's presence you will start to experience a much greater measure of the fire, and people around you will benefit from it, too. But there is a price to pay for the gift you seek." After the man of God spoke over my life I knew I could go deeper. He gave me the desire to pursue God with an even greater zeal.

At that point I began to seek God about how to share the gospel, and as I prayed, fasted and spent time soaking in His presence, He filled me with a brand new compassion for lost souls. As a result I began to reach out in love to those around me, sharing with them out of a brand new and tender heart that they couldn't resist. I was finally beginning to understand what it meant to be a vessel through whom God could pour out His love.

Let me briefly explain so you will understand what it means to pay the price for a gift. The gospel is like food for the believer's heart, and God is the primary provider of that spiritual food. God gives it to someone and that person gives to you at no cost, but it's a whole different situation for the giver. For instance, I can easily feed myself on a daily basis, but in order to provide for many others I have to press in and work for each plate. This process is called carrying our cross, and living for Jesus. Remember that Jesus carried a cross meant for us, so we wouldn't have to. But shouldn't we then be willing to do the same for others? 1 Peter 2:21 tells us: "To this you were called, because Christ suffered for you, leaving you an example that you should follow in his steps."

Once I understood this principle I started fasting and praying, and before long God began revealing Himself to me in spectacular ways. He opened doors that I never thought would open, and He did it just to demonstrate His love for me.

VI
MY FIRST CLASS

I know you will have many questions about seeing in the spirit, but I will try to explain in every possible way as you read on.

I often describe myself as a student, because I choose to learn from everyone and everything to become the unique man God destined me to be. My whole life is about learning. Let me explain why I feel this way.

It was a day like any other day, when, in my regular prayer time, my only focus was for God to use me for His glory. My deepest desire was to understand Him the way He wanted me to. I was ready to give anything away just to learn from Him. I was sitting in my office at work when suddenly I felt a hand on my back. My back was against a chair, and my chair was against a wall so there was no way someone could be behind me. I turned around, and, as expected, there were no one there. If I had to describe the sensation, I would say it felt like a big warm hand that felt a bit heavy. I was wondering what was going on because I felt strange but good sensations in my body. Suddenly I heard a voice speak to me, and it wasn't my boss or a coworker. As a matter of fact, I was alone in my office at the time.

At first, I thought I was going crazy because it was so incredibly real when I recalled the night when I was fifteen. I felt a deep sense of peace. The voice said, "You are one of my chosen ones. I will share many things with you and answer many of your questions." As the voice spoke I saw an angel of God, and the angel came and stood beside me.

As you can imagine I felt surprised and excited at the same time. He said: "Remember when you were young? The voice you heard was the voice of the Father. I am the Spirit, and it was I who baptized you and gave you the gift of tongues the day you called upon My name." Then He said something that sounded strange to me at the time. "The Son of God will appear to you when you are ready. I will always identify myself with peace, joy, and the love of the Lord. The Son can only appear to you when you can identify Him through the Word of God. As you learn the Word of God, we will draw closer to you.

"There will be no confusion between us because I will always make sure to remind you of the blood of the Lamb using these words, "Jesus Christ came to earth and dwelt among men. He died for your sin and through His blood you are free. One day He will come back for you, and we all will be together for eternity."

As he spoke I felt a deep heat penetrate my back and my feet. It was just as He said; there was no confusion in my mind. He continued, "You have been calling upon My name, and I have been answering you, but you were unable to understand my ways. That's why you must learn from Me, for I am gentle in the spirit (see Matt. 11:29). Confusion only comes when there is lack of clarity. The only way you will be able to avoid such confusion is when you get to know Me."

I had never liked to read or write before that time, but after He left, I began to read my Bible like crazy and tried to apply every word to my personal life. I also spent much more time in prayer, and I was suddenly quite sure of everything I did. It wasn't long before my character began to change; the ungodly things I loved that I couldn't let go of, began to fall away from my life.

One day I felt the same sensation of heat on my back, and was overpowered by something, so that words began to appear and move in front of my eyes. I could stop myself from seeing them, and I knew instantly that I was supposed to write for the very first time in my life. I was already quite interested in knowing about the spiritual realm, so I felt excitement rise within me when the Spirit of God began to teach me about it.

Experience with God

I want to share a particular experience with you to show you how great our God is.

My wife and I were living in an apartment and wanted to move elsewhere, so when it came time for our lease to end, we contacted the association and inquired about it. The person said that since they had our deposit, we wouldn't have to pay the last month's rent. We were able to use that money for other things.

Then one day we received an unexpected letter from the association telling us that we must pay the last month's rent after all. But by that time, I had already spent the rent money. Not long afterward, I also received a call from the place where we wanted to move. We had to pay the first and last month's rent plus the security deposit on Wednesday of that same week, to say nothing of the last month's rent that was due for the old place. It was Monday, and I didn't have the money and had no way to get it. The very next day, my wife needed to use the car to run errands, so she decided to take me to work. On the way to work, I heard a voice tell me that my left front tire was in bad shape and to pray that the angel of the Lord would protect us.

I said nothing to my wife about it; instead I prayed in tongues. When I got to work I said, "Honey, my faith has brought me to work. I'm believing that your faith will get you home." Then I explained what the Holy Spirit had said. As she left she began to pray, and a while later she called to say that as she had turned into the parking lot in front of our house the left front tire had blown out.

Remember it was Tuesday, and I needed the money to pay both associations on Wednesday. I sat in my office praying in tongues, and while I was praying the natural man in me wanted to feel isolated and distant from God, and I understood right away that, that was the plan of the enemy. Our enemy is the biggest gambler you could ever imagine. Everything he does is a risk to him, but most of the time he wins because we don't understand his tricks.

As I was praying I understood that the enemy had messed with my tires in order for me not to go to church that Tuesday. I said to myself *that cannot be right because I'm at work.* The Holy Spirit said that it was correct. I felt joy because I knew that once I heard that voice, I was being led in the right direction.

I called a friend to pick me up and he shortly came and got me. I told my boss that I had to leave immediately. I was allowed to leave by grace, so I went home and picked up my wife and we went to a church service. My brother was leading the service, so I texted and told him that I wanted to preach that day and he agreed.

When I got there I took the microphone and opened my Bible to Hebrews 11, and began to preach about faith. It seemed as if I was preaching to a congregation, but the truth is I was preaching to myself because I needed a whole lot of faith. After the message, I said in my heart: "Lord I spoke your Word in obedience, so please demonstrate Your power." After that prayer, the Holy Spirit said to tell everyone to stand, and in five seconds tell them to ask God for whatever they needed. I did what He asked. After the five seconds ended there were so many healings that I couldn't even count them all.

I was excited because I knew God had also answered my prayer though I didn't know how it would manifest. So, I watched as everyone testified, thinking that God would use someone there to provide the money I needed. But nothing happened. After church, I had so much faith that I went to the bank and asked the clerk how much money I had in my account. He said my account was overdrawn by $187.00, and I got a little discouraged because that was my last hope or way to show my faith.

But God had no intention of doing things my way. No longer able to wait on God I felt disappointed so I borrowed my brother's car, and my wife and I went home. I went inside feeling so down and weak that I went to sit on my bed thinking about where I could get that money. I wasn't walking in the spirit or doing things His way anymore. I thought I could do it on my own, although I wouldn't admit it. My actions said it all.

After I'd taxed all my brain cells and found no answers I cried out to the Lord. A still, small voice began to speak, and it said to call the bank. Because I didn't believe it after my earlier bank experience, I said, "I cast you out, devil." Once again the voice said to call the bank. I said, "Listen devil, I already cast you out." A third time the voice repeated the same message, so I pulled out my phone and I called the automated system. I entered the account number, and the voice said, "You have a balance of $5,578.00 in that account." I started to tremble. Then I pressed one to repeat the message again, and it said the same thing. I had planned to go to a check cashing place to borrow whatever we could. But now instead of borrowing the money, we went back to bank. I asked the clerk how much money I had in my account. She said: "You have $5,578.00." I asked, "May I take it?" She said "Yes, it's your money." So I withdrew enough to pay my tithes, and what was needed for the rents and deposits. To this day, I've never even bothered to find out where that money came from. Because this occurred right after Thanksgiving I knew it couldn't be tax return funds. It absolutely had to be God.

I wish I could give you more testimonies because many things happened that proved to me that God is real. It may seem hard to believe that things like that can really happen. But ask yourself this question: "What kind of God is He if He can do those kinds of things?" Maybe the limitations of your faith stop you from seeing this side of God. The truth is that such stunning evidence strengthened my faith and made me want to seek Him even more deeply.

What Does it Mean to See in the Spirit?

This chapter is very important for those who really want to understand the spiritual realm. John 8:32 tells us: "You will know the truth and the truth will make you free." I'm free today because I've met Jesus, not because I've simply heard about Him. Basically, I have to know Him personally in order for me to become free. There has to be an intimate personal encounter for a person to say he actually knows someone.

The Holy Spirit explained it to me this way: Human beings find it very hard to understand the spiritual realm because it is a whole different mindset and mere words cannot fully explain it. Sometimes, we as pastors relate the spiritual realm via stories just to help our people understand. In fact, even Jesus used stories to teach people. But because there are limits to stories told in words, it's important to keep an open mind in order not to limit what God wants to do. As you give Him permission to move in ways you've never seen, He will gradually open a revelation of the spirit.

There are important things that I really want you to know, but first we must understand the spiritual realm via Holy Spirit revelation in order to see into the spirit. To be honest I believed that I had to see things first in order to understand, but He actually said it is necessary to discern the things of the spirit in order for them to manifest. Right after hearing that statement I had questions because such a notion was foreign to my logic. I believed that if I could see something it would make it easier for me to understand, but God's way is not our way, and in fact, He says just the opposite.

I've seen people pray because they want God to open their eyes so they can see in the spirit. But how can one pray for something he can't understand? How will the person recognize it when it comes apart from understanding?

Acts 28:26 says, "Go to this people and tell them: You will listen and you will hear, but you will not understand. You will look and you will see, but you will not understand what you see."

In order for one to see there has to be understanding. My physical eyes can be open, yet in some ways I can still be blind. My ears can be open, yet I can't hear the things of the spirit of God. Our vision depends on our level of understanding. Our understanding is the central processing unit that determines the image we see. So in reality our eyes can't really see. They are only a reflection of our understanding. Say that I have natural eyesight, but I still can't distinguish the difference between the colors red and white. If that is the case I am considered color blind. Matthew 13:12-13 tells us: "Whoever has will be given more, and he will have an abundance. Whoever does not have, even what he has will be taken from him. This is why I speak to them in parables. 'Though seeing, they do not see, though hearing, they do not hear or understand.'"

Let's take for instance: magicians, voodoo priests, witch doctors, and false prophets. They can all see, but without the knowledge and understanding that comes from God, they are all blind because: "The knowledge of the secrets of the kingdom of heaven has been given to you, but not to them" (Matthew 13:11). In conclusion, let me repeat that it is far more important to understand than to see.

Now, you understand why there are false prophets. If they don't have the understanding which comes only through the revelation of the Holy Spirit, they will misinterpret what they see. After I understood this teaching I sought for understanding and knowledge rather than sight. In Hosea 4:6 God Himself said that His people perish because of lack of knowledge.

VII
MY VERY FIRST TRANCE

One day I asked God to take me to heaven because many people I know, including my wife, have had that experience. I continued to ask and expected it to happen, but it never did.

After a time I gave up praying for it. I figured it wasn't in the perfect will of God for me. One day I was getting ready to go to bed, and the Holy Spirit told me not to. I walked around the room instead, though I had no idea why. All of a sudden, I was out of my body (which is very different from being in the spirit). I was in a trance--my very first one. I would imagine someone and the next second I was at that person's house. People of God, the most shocking thing was that the following day I called those people and told them exactly where they were in their house at a certain time the night before and what they were doing, and they were amazed as I was. After a short time of visiting their homes, I found myself in heaven standing next to Jesus.

He asked me to walk with Him. While we were walking He began to show me certain houses, some big and some really small. I asked Him why some of them were so small. At that point He taught me many things I'd never understood.

He said, "My people have too much information, and not enough revelation." I didn't understand what He meant at first. He was looking at the houses as He spoke so I thought He was referring to the houses. He said it was time to stop looking for information and get the revelation.

Though He is an excellent teacher I still didn't get it. So He went on to explain: "There is a meaning behind whatever you see with your natural eyes." People can only give you information, but when the Holy Spirit reveals the revelation about the information, things will finally come alive. The mountain will then hear you speak, the sea will understand your words, and sickness and disease will have to flee."

He said, "Look at these house--what do you see? I said, "I see lots of beautiful houses, some small and some large." He said, "That's good information, but what is the revelation?" I had to admit that I didn't know. He said, "The houses represent human beings on earth, all of them designed by people's understanding of my Father. Some people think He is small, and capable of doing very little, while others think He's big and capable of doing great things. And while it might be easier to understand your perceptions of God that way, on earth everyone thinks and says God is great and able to do amazing things, when deep inside they really don't believe it's true.

"The revelation is the only thing that matters to my Father's kingdom. You need to stop building yourself up with more information, because it will do nothing to bring revelation. It's time that my people get the revelation about the information because nothing supernatural can happen without it."

Many of us go to church, but very few of us know why we were created or what our purpose is. It is almost impossible to live in peace and victory without understanding our destiny, because that is what brings focus and determination. Each of us was created to accomplish something special-- something amazing, and specialization is the only way to our personal success. God has put a unique capability in each one of us that allows us to fulfill our particular destiny.

VIII
MY THIRD VISITATION

My third visitation was in a very dark place. Looking around I asked in confusion, "What is this place?" God's Spirit answered, "It is where the devil takes those who don't wake up in the morning because they allowed themselves to become fresh food." As I walked closer, I began to understand things I'd never understood before. One thing I wish everyone would understand is this: it is not God's desire or intention for any of us to go there.

As I looked around I saw people in that dark place who may have lived better, more luxurious lives than most Christians. But whatever we have comes only by grace, and we should be grateful for what we have. If you are one of those who wake up with pain in your body, and even if there were no pain to begin with, bow your knee and thank Him for allowing you see another day.

The devil works harder and is more devious than we could ever imagine. I have seen farmers sow seeds, but I've never seen them sown in such abundance as the devil sows them. He comes at night when everyone goes to sleep, and his goal is to sow seeds of destruction into people's lives.

The enemy always takes note of everything we say and do. Demon spirits are constantly reporting on everyone's words and deeds. Every evil spirit is responsible for making a report, keeping track of everything. There is one who takes notes before sending it on up the chain of command. When the next spirit receives the report, he will send his workers out to program those people's lives according to words that come out of their mouths and words spoken over their lives, whether good or bad. Then they go around and check your report to see what you have accepted or agreed to and make that happen. (Remember, they can't do anything you haven't agreed to.) Proverbs 13:3 tells us: "He who guards his lips guards his life, but he who speaks rashly will come to ruin."

At night he will come by to sow those terrible seeds in our lives. It could take days, months, and even years before the seed starts to manifest in someone's life or for us to start acting in accord with our words. "The tongue can speak words that bring life or death. Those who love to talk must be ready to accept what it brings" (Prov. 18:21). Things that happen in someone's life are the result of whom he chooses to serve, and words we speak will determine who we are and where we go.

The Power of Words

In Isaiah Chapter 9 the Prophet Isaiah prophesied, speaking of the coming of Jesus over 700 years before His arrival.

Words are spirit and they are alive. In fact, God created the entire world using the words, "Let there be . . ." and God gave us the authority to use those words on a daily basis to bring into being His plans and purposes. In John 6:63b Jesus said, "The words that I speak to you are spirit and they are life." Words are considered to be food, like a magnet that draws every spirit in the spiritual realm, whether good or evil. The spiritual part of every human has to be fed just as his natural part needs physical nourishment. Jesus replied to the devil: (Matt. 4:4): "It is written 'Man does not live on bread alone, but on every word that comes from the mouth of God.'"

Just as sugar attracts ants, bananas attract monkeys, and bones attract dogs, the words that come out of our mouths attract certain spirits. For example: if a person speak words of sickness "I don't feel good." "I doubt if I will ever feel good again." "I will have migraines because my parents did." Such words attract snake spirits and spirits of infirmity that will actually make sure those things come to pass.

Words are among the most powerful weapons available in the spiritual realm. It is the only weapon that can affect both worlds--the spiritual and natural, affecting both humans and spirits. Words can be used to bless or curse anyone or anything. They can either be constructive or destructive in both the spiritual and natural worlds. Shouldn't that be enough reason for us to speak the Word of God since it will attract God's spirit and His angels?

A man's speech always reveals the condition of his heart. A person can only speak according to an inspirational source, originating from either God or the devil. The subject matter in and of itself is not important, because we as human beings don't create anything on our own; we only get inspired and quote what we've heard from a higher source. The people we are today are simply a reflection of what we have spoken into being. We must realize that the words we speak are simply bridges that will lead us to a destiny, whether good or bad.

I used to have dreams where I would be eating in my dreams, but for some reasons I never understood the real meaning of those dreams. That is, until the day I got this teaching and the Holy Spirit showed me that those who are not eating the Word of God will be eating something else—something evil. Every time we spend time reading and meditating on the Word of God, we are feeding out spirits. But when we fail to consume enough of God's Word to keep our spirits strong, we will find ourselves eating whatever poisons the enemy wants to feed us. In other words, we are either eating God's food or poisonous food from the enemy.

John 6:54 quotes Jesus as saying: "Whoever eats my flesh and drinks my blood has eternal life, and I will raise him up at the last day." When we eat the right spiritual food there is no way the enemy will be able to feed us garbage. Matthew 12:43-45 tells us: "When an evil spirit comes out of a man, it goes through arid places seeking rest and does not find it. Then it says, 'I will return to the house I left.' When it arrives, it finds the house unoccupied, swept clean and put in order. Then it goes and takes with it seven other spirits more wicked than itself, and they go in and live there. And the final condition of that man is worse than the first. That is how it will be with this wicked generation."

If the house is unoccupied, he will get more wicked spirits and come and live there. This is what happens to those who do not feed on the Word of God. The enemy will fill them up with all kinds of trash. And oftentimes God is gracious enough to let us know what the enemy is doing is by letting us see ourselves in dreams.

Lord Jesus, I come to You for another mindset

I want to serve You not because I want You to do something for me

But because I was created to serve You, and You deserve all the glory, and honor.

Jesus, please help me to love You the way I should.

You created me, and You gave me breath for which I paid nothing.

You've always taken care of me, no matter what.

Forgive me for being ungrateful, Father, and for not taking the time to really understand the sacrifice of your precious Son, Jesus Christ.

You took in a stranger, an outsider and made me Your child. You took me from the streets, and placed me in a home where You take care of me daily.

Until now I have paid nothing for that, Lord Jesus.

Forgive me, Lord, for my selfishness; I was trying to keep it all for myself when You wanted to give me enough to help others.

Forgive me for waiting so long to share the good news with those who need to hear.

Lord, I haven't done enough to show how much your sacrifice means to me.

From now on I want to demonstrate my love for You in many different ways.

I want my love for You to show, not just through my words, but through my actions.

I want You to be able to say of me, as You said about David, that I am a man after Your own heart.

I want to be able to look deep down inside and say like Paul

That I have fought the good fight of faith, and I take for myself the eternal life You promised me.

It is my pleasure and privilege to go through anything because of Your name,

But be gracious to me, and help me walk away from any situation that would cause me to sin.

From now on I want my actions to reflect Your love.

I want to be like Abraham, Isaac, and Jacob

I will follow Your path and do what the Father says.

Let me love those who hate me with the love of Christ.

Help me to see those who are in need and help them, sharing what You have given me.

Please, Jesus, show me where I am and where I should be.

All I know is that You reward those who love You and follow Your commandments.

Please help me to follow You all the days of my life.

I love you, Jesus.

Amen.

I send fire to every spirit that stands in my way

I send liquid fire to any spirits that are holding onto my blessings.

I destroy every spirit that is working against my destiny.

May my fire increase according to my deep desire to serve God.

So I have enough to destroy Gods' enemies.

God had made me many promises,

And God always keeps His promises, even when I'm unfaithful.

I promise to use everything God has blessed me with to build His kingdom, and to preach the gospel to everyone who will hear it.

I'm going to keep my promise as of today, so it would be a CURSE FOR ANYONE

Or ANYTHING that stands between Your promise to me and my promise to You.

Anyone or anything that tries to hinder or steal Gods' words over my life will be rendered harmless at my feet.

I claim every promise God has made to His children because I, too, am accepted in the beloved, His very own child.

God calls me an anointed one, a chosen one, the best of all I'm an heir of God and a joint heir with Jesus Christ.

Everything that belongs to God belongs to me. In fact, God promised that I will always be the head not the tail. I will lend but not borrow. I am above and not beneath. There will be no lack in my house.

I destroy every spirit that tries to work against Gods' promises in order to make me the tail.

Oh God, anoint my words, empowering them so I can destroy Your enemies, and the enemies of those You love,

Destroying the devil's kingdom, and building your kingdom.

You say that I am the head, while they want me to be the tail

And because Your enemies constantly try to change and distort Your words, God Almighty,

I will use my authority myself to break down every stronghold, set every captive free, and destroy the work of Your enemies.

Oh Lord arise, show them no mercy. Destroy them for Your name's sake.

I pray and seal this prayer with the blood of Your Son, Jesus Christ.

Amen.

CONCLUSION

It is never too late to be who we are destined to be. Nothing is impossible with God. I really want to encourage you to keep seeking God because without Him there is really no power, and no life in us. If you have read this book and prayed this prayer, I believe that something will change in both your natural and spiritual lives. In Jesus' name I prophesy it and it must come to pass.

I thank you for your support and for taking the time read this book. If our time together has blessed you, I hope you will take a moment to go to www.demonstrationministry.org and let us know, or send an email to: jeanswilliam2008@gmail.com. Or you can write or donate to Demonstration Ministries, P.O Box 385 Boynton Beach, Fl 33425, and let us know the book blessed you, and even send us your prayer requests.

We have another powerful book coming soon that will delve deeper into the things of the Spirit. Stay in touch, and we will keep you posted in that regard. God loves you and so do we.

Thanks very much. Be blessed as you seek to go deeper in the things of God.

Apostle Jean Dieudonne

BIOGRAPHY

My name is Jean Sylvio William Dieudonne, and I'm from Haiti. I've been in this country since 2002 due to political reasons (which I talked about in one of the chapter). I was born in July 1983, and I'm called in the Apostolic Ministry at the age of 25. I'm a father of two beautiful daughters, and married to the most beautiful lady. I'm the founder of Demonstration Ministry, a professional musician (piano), a music teacher & writer. I was ordained by Deliverance Ministry, Apostle Gene Moody.

Schools Attended: Wauconda Community College, Blue Ridge Community College, University of Phoenix, and Strayer University.

Apostle Jean S. Dieudonne
www.demonstrationministry.org
P.o. Box 384 Boynton Beach, Fl 33425